How To Wakeboard

Table of Contents

About the Author: Hello and welcome to my book on how to wakeboard! This book is designed for beginner and novice wakeboarders who are looking to learn the basics, such as how to get up, stay up, and actually do something on the water. I've been wakeboarding for over fifteen years and have a wide variety of knowledge on the sport, which I'll gladly share. Throughout the years of boating, you tend to bring a lot of new people up to the lake, which generally results in at least one person asking the ultimate wakeboard question: "how do I do this?". An easy question to ask, but a difficult one to answer.

I began looking for quick guides and books to help answer these questions, but it was to no avail. The most common question is obviously "how do I get up?", but once that question is out of the way, a plethora of others come rolling in. "How do I turn? Do I go outside the wake? How do I get outside the wake? Where should my shoulders/arms be while holding the rope? Do I put my weight forward as if I'm snowboarding, or put my weight back as if I'm skateboarding or surfing?" The questions just keep stacking up, putting up barriers to enjoying the sport.

The books I found were (for lack of better words) terrible, and honestly looked as though someone just went online, copied a bunch of material from others, and slapped together a quick book. Not finding anything of use, I gave up searching. If there was going to be a guide to help people learn how to wakeboard, I was going to have to make it myself, which is exactly what I did. Enjoy!

Quick History

Wakeboarding is now the fastest growing watersport in the world, and that says a lot. The sport, which until recently was only seen as an activity, got its roots in 1985 with the invention of the skurfboard and skurfing. The man credited with the invention (a mix between waterskiing and surfing, hence the silly name) was Tony Finn. The skurfer looked like a small surfboard with the addition of foot bindings.

The boards were heavy, but would still float and were designed for carving on the wake. The bindings were nothing fancy, but rather simple pull back elastic (for the heels) or sandalstyle velcro straps that went over the top of your foot. The board had a pointy nose and flat back with three skags (more commonly known as fins) on the back for stability. With that structure, an obvious flaw in early skurfing was that you could only go one direction and not turn fakie (a term for your alternate foot forward, or 180 degrees from your normal stance). It was a great start, having at that time waterskiing was still king.

It did not take long for skurfing to catch on and once it did, it really took off! The first double ended boards were introduced, poles and towers started showing up on ski boats, wakes were getting bigger, and boats were getting heavier. Today you rarely see anyone out on an old singleended skurfer (although you can occasionally find vintage ones for sale on eBay), but you see countless lightweight double end boards, all of which push the boundaries for what riders can do behind a boat. The current technology (2015) is boards that are flexboards, allowing riders to physically bend the board as they are riding. It sounds crazy, but it's true! Granted, it is not much of a flex as the integrity of the board is still solid, however for riding rails and parks it is bringing the sport to new heights (literally).

Equipment and Accessories

Let's talk about getting started. Luckily, there are only a few key items that are needed, the biggest being a boat. My assumption is that you either have or have access to a ski boat, so I will skip past this part for now. I will be talking more about boats in the later chapters, introducing things such as driving patterns and ideal setups. You will, however, need a board, or at least have access to a board. What type of board you ask? To start, the bigger the better. I'm not saying to go out and buy a gigantic wakeboard, but if you are new and there are a few different size boards on the boat, I would suggest going with a larger option. The reason is surface area. The more area the board will cover, the more stable you will be once standing. Think of surfing for a minute (if you have ever surfed), you will always start out on a longboard as they are big and stable. It is only when you are looking for more control and faster turning that you move up to a short board. It is easier to get up on a longboard while surfing than a short board; the same is true with wakeboards.

An often overlooked element of wakeboarding is the rope. What type of handle should I have and what length should it be?   Regarding the handle type, I will leave that to your discretion, as it really does not matter that much for a beginner. Make sure the handle floats (as nearly all do), else you will have a difficult time finding it once you fall, but other than that, find something that you feel you can hang onto (and won't rip up your palms) and you will be fine. The length of the rope is a much more loaded question and takes one really important factor into consideration: the speed in which the boat is pulling the rider. A beginner rider is going to want to go slow, and I mean *really* slow (1015 mph). This is fine for anyone getting up their first few times, but is putting the rider at a huge disadvantage if they remain at that speed. They will get comfortable at that speed and not want to exceed it.

Each boat performs a little differently, however the ideal speed you will find is going to be between 2023 mph.

Advanced riders may take it up to 25+ mph, but I would not recommend this speed. My ideal speed for the boat I use is somewhere between 2122 mph (depending on how well I am doing that day).

The reason the boat speed matters so much is because it determines how long your rope should be. Most ropes will come 90+ feet standard, but that is way too long, especially if you are a beginner. Shorten the rope to around 60 feet to start. If you want to see how it looks behind your boat, throw the rope out (after attaching to your pole or tower, of course) and test how the rope handle looks in comparison to the wake. You will see on either side of the wake, there is a clear point where the wake turns from a nice, smooth, rounded edge to a pile of crashing white water (think of a wave at the beach where it eventually closes out and there is nothing left but white water splashing around. You do not want to ride in the white water, so the rope handle should be no longer than where the white water begins. Again, depending on the boat type and speed, your rope length is going to vary.

The nice part is that the length will not change too much between rider to rider, however throughout the day chances are there will be a number of rope length changes.

Anything else? Well, there are plenty of accessories to go over, but I will not spend too much time on them. Below are a few key items that you will come across and information on each one:

- **Life Jacket**: wear one! It does not matter how good you are, by law you must wear a jacket while being towed behind a boat. The pros even wear these (most of the time), so take a note from their book and play it safe.
- **Rash Guard**: not essential, but will keep your life vest from rubbing up against your skin. For the fairskinned folk, it will also act as an excellent way to keep from getting sunburned, or to help grow your farmer tan (whichever you prefer).
- **Gloves**: not essential, but a good way to keep your palms from growing giant calluses or blisters. Personally I do wear gloves out on the water, but many people choose not to.

- **Soap**: highly controversial out on lakes, but most boaters will have a small liquid soap container on board. Wakeboarders use soap to help slide into (older model) bindings that do not have laces or ties. Environmentally, it is not healthy to have a ton of soap residue floating around in the water, but if you have ever tried squeezing your feet into some older model bindings, it is completely understandable.

- **Orange Flag**: as a boat owner or user, you will have to have someone in the boat hold (or secure) the flag whenever a person, object, or even just the rope is in the water. The flag is an indicator to other boaters that there is something in the water and they should keep their distance when passing.

As for anything else, there are literally hundreds of little gadgets and devices sold to help your wakeboarding experience (camera holders, autorope snappers, mounts, flag holders, etc), but these are all extras that are definitely not critical for wakeboarding. Now that all the gear is

handled, let's get to the main focus of the book and go over how to actually get started.

The Basics: How To Get Up

At this point, you've got what you need, you're out on the water, and you're ready to go in. Do not panic! This next part will walk you through step by step on how to make it look as though you know what you are doing and more importantly, how to get up.

Before we get into the exact method for getting up, there is one critical item that you must know: your stance. There are two types of stances: Regular (which is your left foot forward) or Goofy (which is your right foot forward). Most boards these days are setup with the stance in somewhat of a duck placement, meaning it shouldn't matter what direction the front of the board is in as both feet are equally pointed outward, however for our situation, we should know. If the rider has experience on a skateboard, surfboard, snowboard, or any board for that matter, they will know which is their strong foot forward and it will be the same for the wakeboard. However, some riders will not know their stance and with all the pressure of having to get up on a wakeboard, will not know which feels correct. When this happens, there are a few nifty tricks to help figure out the proper stance, which I've listed below:

- Ask: "if you were to run full speed to a frozen lake to slide across the top of it in your shoes, which foot

  would you want in front?" The foot you would put in front will be the foot you want in front for wakeboarding.
- Ask: "if you had to jump as high as you could, which foot would you plant to make the jump?". The foot that they would plant would be the riders back foot in wakeboarding.
- Have the person stand up with their feet together and without telling them, simply give them a little nudge forward. Look at their feet to see which one they instinctively put forward to catch their balance. Whichever foot goes forward is the front foot for riding.

If all else fails, simply try one way and see how it feels. If it feels wrong after a few tries, you can always switch the bindings and try the other direction.

The process to follow when it's your turn to go should be as follows: put on your vest (in the boat), setup your rope (unless it's already set), grab the board you are using, carry the board to the back platform (being careful not to ding or hit any part of the boat, a common mistake!), put the board down on the back platform, sit down on the back of the boat end and slide your feet into the bindings, take a deep breath, grab the rope handle (or throw it out), and hop in the water.

Once you are in the water, the boat will slowly start driving away from you. You will notice that someone will be holding up the aforementioned orange flag, which is good. Your main objective at this point is to get ahold of the rope handle and to be facing the boat. A *very* common mistake is to let the boat spin you around so you have your back or side to the boat. You need to be firm and make sure what you are in a sitting back position (such as one you would be in sitting on a couch tilted back a bit) with your knees bent right up to your chest. The board will be right in front of you and should be perpendicular with the water. Your elbows should be on the outside of your knees with both hands gripping the handle right in front of your chest. You will be sitting back, crunched into somewhat of a ball. The boat will continue to drive away at a slow pace until there is no more slack. The boat will let up on the throttle, but remember boats do not have any brakes, and even when the throttle is let up and in neutral, the boat's inertia will keep the boat moving forward, essentially continuing to slowly pull you. Again, you will have to be firm and confident in the water making sure that you are not being thrown around by the boat. Some have described this part as "pulling back the boat", which is a hard thing to visualize, but is what you are trying to do. There should be no slack in the rope and at this point, things are about to get real.

"Hit it!" is the traditional boating lingo for "OK, I'm ready for you to start pulling me up now.", but any phrase can be used. Over the years I have heard people yell things such as "Go!", "Ok!", or my personal favorite: "Booya!" You may also use a headnod (as most advanced riders do), however for learning purposes, it is best to have a verbal code for the driver to know you are ready.

Once signaled, the driver will hit the throttle fairly hard to pull you up. Do not have the driver slowly pull you out of the water, as you will not get up this way. The worst approach (that I have seen over and over) is a new rider wanting to be dragged along at 5 mph and for the driver to slowly go faster and faster. This will not work. You need to be pulled out of the water as quickly as possible. It sounds fast, but remember, boats are not race cars, these are heavy floating vessels starting up from a near standstill. Even if the throttle was pushed the whole way, it would still take 3+ seconds for the boat to really get going, plenty of time to comfortably get up. But once the boat starts going, what do you do as the rider?

You will hear the engine of the boat and feel your arms being pulled forward slightly. As the board is perpendicular with the horizon, you will feel some water resistance in your legs, all of which is a good sign. Make sure to keep your arms tucked back to your chest with both hands on the rope. Do not let go for any reason, and you will want to especially if you do not feel balanced. A common mistake is to let the boat pull your arms in front of you too far or to try with one hand, however this will throw off your center and make it very difficult to get up. You want to remain in the crunched ball position, holding your arms tight and using your bent knees to handle any turbulence. You are still in the water for the first few seconds as the boat starts going, which is good. You do not want to try to stand up too quickly, or else you will either sink or topple over. You want to hold back and when the boat has picked up enough speed (generally 23 seconds after it starts moving forward), you want to simply roll yourself up.

The best analogy for getting up is to be pulled out of a rocking chair. This has worked countless times when training a new rider to get up for the first time. Imagine you are sitting in a rocking chair with a rope in front of you. When the rope gets pulled, imagine you are first pulled forward slightly, and then pulled up and out of the rocking chair. This can often be hard to visualize when you are actually out on the water, so I would encourage you to engrain this in your mind now and actually practice on a chair ahead of time. While sitting, pull your knees up to your chest, hold your hands in front, and rock forward so that you are standing up. A major plus on getting up with newer model boats is that they have the rope connected to the highest part of the tower or pole, which makes it easier to be pulled up (imagine the old days when the rope was connected about a foot over water level). Do not worry about the orientation of the board at this point. When standing up for the first few times, the board will appear to be perpendicular to the boat instead of straight aligned forward. This is OK, trust me. The board will automatically shift and turn to be facing the boat. Sound weird? It is, but it works. As you become more advanced, you will notice yourself turning the board at the time of getting up, but for now it is better to not even notice the board orientation and to keep it perpendicular to the boat.

That's really all there is to it. It's not so hard to get up on a wakeboard and it certainly sounds more difficult than it actually is. It may take you a few times, but you will get the hang of it so long as you continue to think of yourself as a crunched up ball being pulled out of a rocking chair.

Once your are up, the first task is done, but there is a whole lot more to learn.

Common Problems with Getting Up

As easy as I just made the process sound, many people still do struggle with getting up, especially if they are not used to board sports in general. Even those who have great balance and are incredibly athletic can often times struggle to get the technique down. A close family friend, who is very well coordinated, once tried thirty times in a row to get up, determined to 'get it' before the end of the trip. On his thirtyfirst attempt, and after countless tips and encouraging remarks from the boat, he finally did it. The beauty was after he got up that one time, he was able to replicate and could get up each of his proceeding tries. However, there were few tries after that initial stands for that trip, as failing thirty times in a row can do a number on your arms as well as the attitude of those others on the boat patiently awaiting their turn.

Just as people say once you learn how to ride a bike you never forget, the same can be applied to wakeboarding. But how do you get it right to begin with? Below is a list of common problems I have seen when teaching new riders how to get up for the first time:

- *The board sinks with water going over the top as soon the boat starts going.* This means you are not sitting far enough back in the water. Lean back a bit more and make sure your knees are bent enough. The

  board should be at least one third buoyant out of the water where you can see the top of your bindings.

- *You try standing up and sink.* This means the boat driver is not punching the throttle fast enough in the initial start. Have the driver really hit the gas when they start going to make sure there is enough power to pull you out.

- *You do not get up and the rope handle shoots back all the way to the boat.* This is kind of a funny one, but it can also be a pretty dangerous situation as those handles hurt. It is also a great way to break the rope. The reason this is happening is due to the rider tugging back on the handle before realizing that the boat is more powerful and pulling the handle out of the rider's hand. The way to fix this is to not fight the boat and allow your arms to move forward slightly with the pull of the boat. Do not let your arms all the way out, but do allow them some flexibility.

- *The boat keeps pulling but you never make it out of the water.* If this happens, you are holding back too much. Let the boat pull you out as though the boat is pulling you out of a chair. You are fighting back too much, and it's a balance of not too much give or take when it comes to working with the boat.

- *You try to stand up but get pulled over.* This happens when there is too much give and not enough pull back

   on the rope. If your arms get pulled all the way forward and your torso does not move with them, then the only thing is for your upper half to be tugged too far forward, resulting in a faceplant, which is not fun.

- *You stand up but fall backwards instantly.* Believe it or not, this is not a huge deal and if this is happening then you are a few tries away from getting the technique down. More than likely once you are standing the board is not automatically turning to the correct direction. You may need to work on shifting your back foot once you feel you are out of the water and leaning further forward.

Fundamentals: What To Do Once Up

Getting up on a wakeboard is a great thing, however once you are up, you will then wonder what to do. Luckily, there are only a few things to keep in mind to ensure you have a good time and do not end up pulling any muscles. Below is the mental checklist you should go through once you are standing up:

- *Is your back straight?* This will be the hardest thing for most people who are just starting out. Naturally you will arch your back forward, but this is not good. Just as weight lifters focus on form and keeping their backs straight (in the natural back arch), so should you while wakeboarding. To see for yourself, find a fullbody mirror and act as though you are standing on a wakeboard. First, lean forward (towards the imaginary boat) and see how that looks. Next, stand up straight with your back in a more natural arch and see the difference. It is a much better look.

- *Are your arms bent slightly (not fully extended), holding the rope stomach to chest height?* By default on the first few tries, the rope will be around eye level and fully extended out. This will pull your back to a curved shape and will make it harder to control. You want the handle close to your body and below your head.

- *Are your knees bent slightly?* If you want your knees to survive some of the choppy water you will encounter, you are going to need to make sure you keep your knees bent as your shock absorbers. Be aware that if you bend your knees too much, you look

   very silly on the board, however a slight bend is essential.

- *Is your weight centered over the middle of the board?* Unlike other board sports where your weight is either on your front foot (snowboarding) or back foot (surfing and skateboarding), with wakeboarding your weight should be right in the middle. To help position yourself, do a few "water bounces" where you push up as though you are doing a tiny hop on land. After a few consecutive hops, if you are still standing, your weight will be in the correct position.

- *Are your bathing suit pant legs rolled down?* Take a minute and check, as getting pulled out of the water can often times roll them up pretty far. It's a great way to work on the upper leg tan, but a bad way to look like you know what you are doing. If they are rolled up, do yourself a favor and use a free hand to quickly roll them down (the boat passengers will appreciate the gesture).

You are now up and standing in good form, so what's next? This is where the book gets into the more intermediate section and some of the items that are listed below will be a bit tough for beginners. Do not feel discouraged if you cannot do everything listed, rather use this as a checklist (going from top to bottom) to master each one. In the following section I will also be providing a list of tricks to start with, which can also be used as a checklist to mark your progress.

- Hold the rope with one hand (your front hand)
- Carve back and forth within the wake
- Go outside the wake (both toeside and heelside)
- Turn as wide as possible
-

Carve against the outside of the wake

Once you are able to do all of these, you are ready to take your wakeboarding to the next level and start thinking about tricks (the reason most people want to wakeboard to begin with).

Beginner Trick List

Alright, so you can now stand up and carve around the wake a little, very impressive. But the true test comes when you have a boat full of passengers waiting to see what you are going to do next. So what do you do? Here's a list of the best beginner tricks to master to not only impress spectators, but also get you more familiar with the board. The list below is ordered from easy to more intermediate and all should be done before moving into any more difficult tricks. All of the beginner tricks are known as "surface tricks", as the board never leaves the water.

A few terms to know before we get started, that will help out immensely when reading the trick list:

- **Backside or Heelside**: think of this as the "back of the binding/boot side". Whenever the term 'backside' is used, it refers to the direction the board is facing.

- **Frontside or Toeside**: just as with backside, this can be seen as the opposite as the front of the binding/boot side.

- **Grab**: this simply means grasping the board for any amount of time (the longer the better in most cases).

- **OffAxis**: occasionally you will hear about something being done 'offaxis', which refers to the orientation of your body while in the air. If it appears the rider is crooked in the air, chances are they are performing a trick offaxis, which makes any trick slightly more difficult.

- **180**: moving the board 180 degrees.

- **360**: one full rotation around (two 180s).

- **540**: one and a half rotation around (three 180s).

- **720**: two full rotations (four 180s).

- **900**: two and a half rotations (five 180s).

- **1080**: three full rotations (six 180s). This is the highest rotation any rider can get to, although there are stories of riders surpassing this threshold.

- **Handle Pass**: the rider passes the handle behind their back from one hand to the other.

- **To Blind:** the rider lands with the rope wrapped around their back instead of passing the handle.

- **Wrapped:** when the rider has the rope wrapped around their back when riding they are are going to perform a wrapped trick. It allows a rider to spin without doing a handle pass.

Alright, on to the actual beginner trick list. Additional tricks have been provided by the site Wakeboarder.com and Wikipedia.org, which are both excellent references for trick guides:

- **One Hander**: Rider holds the rope with their strong side hand (hand that is in front). For example, if you are riding goofy (right foot forward), you would hold with your right hand while keeping good form.
- **Surf Carve:** Rider cuts back and forth in the wake in a surfcarving fashion.

- **Backside Start:** Rider gets up in a backside position where the backside is facing the boat.
- **Butterslide:** Rider turns the board frontside 90 degrees and grinds the wake.

- **Butterslide 180:** Same as regular butterslide but with an additional 90 degree rotation in the same direction.
- **Backside Butterslide:** Rider turns the board backside 90 degrees and grinds the wake.
- **Backside Butterslide 180:** Rider turns the board backside 90 degrees and grinds the wake. Rider then grabs the handle with opposite hand and does another 90 degree turn in the same direction.
- **NoHander:** Rider puts handle between knees, then lets go with both hands.
- **Surface 180:** A 180 degree turn on the surface of the water.
- **Pop 180**: A 180 degree rotation above the surface of the water.

- **Surface 360:** A 360 degree turn on the surface of the water.

- **Nothing Butterslide:** Rider puts handle between knees while in a butterslide.

- **Perez:** Rider carves outside of the wake and slides into a surface 360.

- **Powerslide:** Board is turned backside 90 degrees in the flats. Fins are broken loose. If done correctly, it creates a huge spray (which is sometimes called a 'roostertail', an old waterski term).

How To Get Air

After a few times going back and forth over the wake and getting a feel for the board, you are going to want to start addressing the wake to actually get some air. Hitting the wake takes your riding to the next level and I would reserve this practice until you are comfortable on your board and can maneuver around in complete control.

Some instructional sites that I visited have riders 'go for it' and attack the wake at full force on their first few tries. I disagree with this methodology as it only results in a major spill and the rider not enjoying their first experience with the wake. Instead, the best way to begin working with the wake is to work on your approach, but to not actually get leave the water as you reach the wake. Using our knees as shock absorbers, allow the wakeboard to cut through the wake, working on this approach from both sides. Let's start out by discussing how to approach the wake:

- When the water is calm, cut out as far as you can to your strong side of the wake (with your back to the wake).
- You will need to really lean into your cut to get far outside of the wake, as the boat's natural pull is to have you directly behind the boat. Many will lose their balance at this point, which is why it is important to get used to this feeling early on.

- When you are outside of the wake as far as you can get, stand back up at your normal stance, keep your hands tucked/low, and look at the wake. You want to only approach the wake when it is nice and ramplike with no white water. If the ramp is not there, it will only

  make it more difficult to learn, so it is worth waiting until the wake is set properly.

- Cut in hard, shooting yourself back towards the middle of the boat with both hands firmly holding the rope handle.

- When you arrive at the wake, normally this would be the time to allow the ramp (wake) to throw you into the air, however for our learning experience, bend your knees as you go over the wake and continue your way to the other side of the wake.
- After a few tries of having your knees absorb the shock of the wake and not getting any air, move forward with having your knees absorb a little less and letting the board leave the water. Keeping your speed up, allow the wake to launch your body through the air, remaining in control the whole time (or as much as possible). The first few tries will be awkward, and you will feel completely out of control, however after a handful of tries you will start to get the hang of it.

Now that you are in the air, we need to
work on landing. Landing incorrectly
can cause some serious
injuries, so you want to be sure to land
on your feet with your knees bent. Try to
keep your hands/arms at your waist
level (this helps with keeping control).

The main goal is not to do anything fancy in the air, but rather to make it to the other side of the wake. Just as the initial side acted as a launch ramp, the other side of the wake acts as a soft landing pad. Not making it all the way across or overshooting the wake will have you landing on flat water. While that may sound nice, it is a much more impactful landing and hard on your joints.

Really take some time to work on jumping wake to wake from both directions. You will naturally want to start on your strong side, however when you get into more intermediate tricks, you will have to be able to clear the wake from both sides so you may as well practice now.

From a personal standpoint, I did not spend much time on my weak side and now am regretting that decision. When you have both sides down and you are able to clear the wake in complete control, move on to more intermediate tricks!

Intermediate Trick List

Now that the beginner tricks have been mastered and you can now address the wake to catch some airtime, it is time to move on to the more intermediate tricks. All but a few of these tricks are done in the air (where most of the action takes place) and usually involve some sort of grab. As mentioned before, a grab is simply using your hand (which hand depends heavily on the trick) and gripping an area of the board. In almost all cases, the longer you can hold the board the better.The tricks here are sure to turn some heads, so make sure you attempt them all when you are ready!

- **Body Slide:** Rider lies back onto the water.

- **Tumble Turn:** Rider lays back on water, board is taken out of water and above the head, body is spun around backside and the rider stands back up onto feet.
- **Tail Grab:** Rear hand, grabbed on tail of board.

Nose Grab: Lead hand, grabbed on tip of the board.

- **Mute Grab:** Lead hand, toeside grab, between feet.
- **Palmer Grab:** Lead hand, front heelside grab with a slight twist of the body for style.

Canadian Bacon Grab: Rear hand, toeside grab, between feet, through legs.

- **Chicken Salad Grab:** Front hand, heelside grab, between feet, through legs, arm is twisted, lead foot is boned out.
- **Crail Grab:** Rear hand, front toeside grab, back leg is pushed out.
- **Indy Grab:** Rear hand, toeside grab, between feet.
- **Indy Nosebone Grab:** Rear hand, toeside grab, between feet, push out your front leg and point it back to where you came from.
- **Lien Air:** Lead hand, heelside grab, board pushed in front of rider, back leg pushed out.

- **Melancholy Grab:** Lead hand, heelside grab, between feet, front leg is pushed out.

- **Method / Method Air:** Lead hand, heelside grab, between feet, board is brought up to waist.

- **Stalefish Grab:** Rear hand, heelside grab, between feet.

- **Tai Pan Grab:** Lead hand, toeside grab, between feet through legs.

- **Nuclear Grab:** Rear hand, front heelside grab, back leg pushed out.

- **Roast Beef Grab:** Rear hand, heelside grab, between feet, through legs.

- **Seatbelt Grab:** Rear hand grabs the nose of the board across the rider's body, as though they are putting on a car seatbelt.

- **Japan Air:** Lead hand grab in front of front foot while board is brought up so it's perpendicular to the water.

- **Slob Grab:** Lead hand, front toeside grab, back leg pushed out, board rotated 180 while in the air.

- **Stiffy:** Board is brought out flat in front of the rider. Typically done with an Indy or Roast Beef grab.

- **Shifty:** Term for while in the air, the board is shifted 90 degrees in one direction and then shifted back in the opposite direction.

- **Rewind:** Term for an aerial where the rider does a shifty one way, then back the other, then spins back in the direction of their initial shifty.

- **180**: In the air, switching your front foot to your back foot. This can be done either toeside or heelside.

- **360**: Rotating yourself one full rotation (360 degrees) while in the air. Often times this will include a handle pass, but the rider may also start with the handle wrapped or land to blind instead. Quick tip for handle passes: really pull the rope into your back and keep it close when passing from one hand to the next.

Backroll: A backflip (done in the same style as you would if doing a backflip on a trampoline).

Master these tricks and you will be ready to move to more complex tricks. The beauty of mastering the different grabs is because the more advanced tricks usually combine a grab with an invert or spin (or both). Knowing exactly how to do the different grabs will set you up well for attempting some of the bigger tricks out there.

Remember, it's only water you are landing on, and it's not so bad when you fall (although faceplants definitely do hurt, so try to stay away from those).

Boat Driving: Patterns and Etiquette

The driver of the boat has just as much to do with the success of your wakeboarding as your you do. That's because the driver shapes the wake, decides on directions to the calm water, and pulls at adjusting speeds. Sure, the rider can help out the driver by pointing where they want to go and by using the 'thumbsup or thumbsdown' for faster or slower speeds, but the rider is not the one in control.

There are also very specific boat driving patterns and etiquette that should be respected out on the water. Follow these simple rules and you will not have other boats yelling at you as you drive by:

- *How to get the rope back to a fallen rider.* I will start out by saying there are a lot of wrong ways to do this, which I will get into in the next bullet point, and really only one correct way. The process is as follows:
  - When the rider has fallen, someone in the boat raises the orange flag (to signal the rider is down) and notifies the driver that someone is 'down' (often times this word is yelled out).
  - The driver lets up on the throttle, slowing the boat down to a near standstill. Let the wake push through and wait until it has passed.
  - At a slow pace, turn the boat around (either direction is fine) 180 degrees and begin driving back directly towards the rider.

- When you are nearing the rider, swing the boat around the rider or snake the rope past them. You should get close, but not too close (as you do not want to hit or run over the rider).
- The rope will either be within arms distance of the rider, or they will simply have to reach up when it goes over their head. Again, the handle floats, so at worst case scenario, the rider may have to paddle a little to the rope handle.

- *Powerturn.* Simply put, you do not want to do these while driving a boat. A powerturn is when the rider falls and the boat driver decides that the best thing to do is to turn the boat around and 'power' through the existing wake with a heavy throttle. While it works great for picking up the rider (you get to them a lot faster), it is awful for the water quality, as it really chops up it up. Full disclosure, it is difficult to follow the rule of 'no powerturns' and I am guilty of this myself. However, if other boaters see you making these turns to pick up your rider, especially if it is a small lake with not a lot of good water left, they will let you know what they think of your powerturn.

- *What happens if another boat is coming towards me?* This will happen, but just as you would handle a car passing by on a road, the same rules apply. Try to 'stay right' on a passing and give plenty of room between boats (especially if there is a rider in the water). If a car passing on a road is separated by one car length, the appropriate boat distance would be 34 times that. Simply put, you want to give a good amount of space between boats when passing.

- When passing a boat, general boater etiquette is to give a small waive or tip of the hat to the passing boat driver. This signifies that you are aware of them and that you respect the distance they are giving during the pass.

- Once you have passed the boat, if there is a wake that the other boat created, you do not want to stay parallel to this wake and have it hit your boat from the side. Instead, the best move is to slowly angle towards the wake and cut through anywhere from a 4590 degree angle. This helps get through the other boat wake and staying in control the whole time. If there is a rider behind you while you are cutting through a wake, or just some rough water ahead, the universal sign to signal to the rider is your arm straight out with your palm flat (signaling flat water), then raise your arm up and down to signal the water ahead being rough.
- *Turning the boat with a rider.* It is inevitable that eventually you will have to turn the boat around while

pulling a rider. The good news is that this is very easy to do. Instead of making a tight turn as you might do while turning without a rider, make a more rounded turn (bigger curve) so that the rider is able to stay in control the whole time. Keep the speed constant (do not slow down or speed up unless you need to), as the rounded turn will keep a consistent speed going throughout. Note that if you are turning left and make a tight turn, the rider will either sink if they are on the left side of the wake or be shot out to the right if they are on the right side of the wake. The old rule people would reference from the days of tubing behind boats is that when the boat turns and the tube is shot across the wake, the tube is going double the speed of the boat. I cannot say for sure how accurate this statement is, but I can tell you it sure feels like it!

Pattern wise, there are really only a few things that a boat driver needs to know. The best thing to do is to look for the calm (glassy) water and to drive in as straight of a line as possible. Often times, a cove or outlet near the edges of lakes work as the best places to pull a rider as the shore acts as a breaker for the passing wakes. As you get more advanced, there is one driving pattern that is very well known in the wakeboarding community and will surely come up: the doubleup.

The doubleup is tricky, but not that bad when you know what you are doing as a driver. A doubleup is when the driver does a wide turn and goes back around to drive straight through the original wake. By doing this, the initial wake rolls into the new wake, creating one gigantic wake that can often be close to double the original wake size.

Timing is important for the rider as they will have to address the wake right at the correct moment to make sure the two wakes are perfectly aligned, but more important is the driver coming through the wake at a 90 degree angle (straight through it). Most boats produce a set of three wakes (or rollers as they are called). When going in for a double up as a rider, you have a choice to go for the first, second, or third roller. When you are first starting out, definitely go for the first one, as you will not have to deal with passing through a roller and it is the best place to start getting used to the new size of the wake.

Most professionals will launch from the second roller as it is generally slightly bigger, but for our purposes the first one is the way to go and the best place to start. As a driver, the biggest thing to remember is to go straight through your prior wake at the 90 degree angle, as even the slightest angle change will affect the wake structure.

Courtesy on the water is to only perform doubleup driving patterns when there is plenty of space and no nearby boats that would have to deal with the extra wakes you are generating.

Creating the Perfect Wake

Wakeboard boats these days are mainly built for two things: comfort and a perfect wake. Ironically, ski boats used to brag about how little of a wake they could produce as water skiing requires as small of a wake as possible. Now that wakeboarding is in the limelight, the focus is on creating big, heavy, launch-ramp looking wakes for riders to get some great height. Trust me, riding behind a boat with a well crafted wake is a much different experience than riding behind a normal wake.

The easiest way to have a clean, builtup wake is to have a newer boat that comes fully loaded with all the bells and whistles, but even then, there are plenty of tweaks to be done before the ideal situation is found. Unfortunately there is not a single formula for creating a wake (as all boats are slightly different), but below I will go over a few aspects that really affect the wake structure.

Boat Weight. Probably one of the most important factors in the overall size of the wake, the actual weight of the boat will make a big difference. In fact, newer model boats will come with specific compartments designed to hold ballast sacks to weigh the boat down (older models use this thing called "people" to help increase the weight). If your boat does not have ballast bags, they can be found at most boat stores and can be thrown anywhere on board, but placement definitely matters.

Yes, to make things even more complicated, you cannot just fill the boat with weight and call it a day, you have to balance out the new weight of the boat. The general rule for most riders is the 60/40 rule of "60% of the weight in the back and 40% up front", which I would recommend following to start. The more weight you have in the front, the more of a rampy and clean surface wake will develop. The more weight in the back will result in a steeper wake but also much more whitewash (requiring a faster speed to keep the shape).

As for how much weight, when talking about ballast bags, pounds are used as the unit of measurement and the bags will come in different fill levels and capacities. Most intermediate to advanced riders would use around 8001,000lbs in the back and 500-600lbs in the front.

Sound like a lot of weight? It is. Will this lower your gas mileage on the water? Big time. Will it create a nice ramp for launching a rider? Definitely.

Wedges and Plates. High end wakeboard boats these days have what are known as wedges or plates (depending on the boat brand) and they are exactly what they sound like. They are hydrofoil devices that drop down behind the prop and act as a plow (think farming). The system creates downward force which pulls the back of the boat lower into the water, thus creating a bigger wake. Older boats do not have an equivalent, but for the most part there is not a need for a wedge in the early stages of your wakeboarding career. As you get more advanced it will start to make a huge difference, but for now it will be easier to learn the basics without also having to deal with an enormous wake to clear.

Trim. Adjusting the trim of your boat while pulling a rider is a great way to make subtle adjustments to the wake. The trim causes the front of the boat to rise or lower by the press of a button. By default, start with the trim all the way down and toggle up as you shape the wake. Although adjustments of the trim will not make a major difference in the size of the wake, it is great to use to clean up a wake that needs a final tweak.

The Art of Falling

This may sound silly, but there is both a good way and a bad way to fall on a wakeboard. The main objective is not to fall at all, but if you do, there are a few things you can do to make the way down a little less harsh.

On the record I will state that falling while wakeboarding can, in fact, hurt. Yes, you are falling on water, which does sound soft, but you are falling on water going 20+ mph with your body potentially twisted around. Depending on the angle of your body and what part of your body is hitting the water first can make a huge difference in the level of pain that you endure. Following the below tips on falling will help quite a bit, especially when learning a new trick:

- *Drop the rope.* Any wakeboard forum or magazine will tell you otherwise, but it is one of the better ways to avoid major spills. The reason most other sources will say to hang on at all costs have to do with people using the rope drop as an excuse and not fully committing to a trick. The counter is that some of the falls that happen while holding on can put a rider off wanting to ever attempt the trick again. For example, I have had the wind knocked out of me after falling bellyfirst on the wake on a raley attempt that I knew I was not going to land (but held on to the rope anyway). Floating on your back in an open lake without the ability to breathe correctly is not a fun experience, and since the incident, I have been reluctant to practice the trick.

- *Lead with your arms.* You will have about a halfsecond to react to the fact that you are falling, so these tips might be hard to remember at the time, but leading a fall with your arms (when possible) is a great trick to help distribute the weight of the fall and make the impact less severe.
- *Spot your landing, even if you are not going to make it.* Regardless of the trick, your eyes should always be looking for the landing as soon as possible. This is especially important if you are not going to land your

attempted trick. The reason is because when you see where you are going to land, your brain is able to make a quick decision on the best way to protect your body (which hopefully includes dropping the rope and trying to lead the fall with your arms). You will unconsciously already do this. Imagine trying to clear the wake with your eyes closed and how difficult that attempt would be. Your brain wants to know what's coming up, so give your brain a break and help it out by spotting where you are going to land (or fall).

- *Watch out for the board.* The wakeboard itself is a dangerous thing, and it is strapped right to your body! Common board hits include your arms hitting the board, your head hitting the board (note: some people

  wear helmets because of this possibility), or your body landing on the board upon impact. How do you avoid the board hitting your body? The best way is to always be mindful of the wakeboard and to stay in control during a fall. Keep your legs strong and do not let the board shoot off wherever it wants to. It is difficult, but staying in control of the board will help with your overall safety.

- *Do not faceplant.* An obvious one, right? No one actively seeks out a faceplant, yet they still happen out on the water all the time. If you are going to faceplant, train yourself to exhale through your nose on each fall. This will at least mitigate the risk of water shooting up your nose, making the experience even worse.

That's It!

You made it! At this point, you should have a firm understanding of the basics of wakeboarding and a good idea of how to get started. Like most things in life, practice is the best way to improve your skill, so try some of the techniques and tips described in this book and you will be a pro in no time. Focus on things such as keeping your back in its natural arch, bending your knees slightly to act as shock absorbers, and spotting your landing during a crash. You will find that over time the methodology described in this book does actually work and that you can in fact wakeboard the correct way. Not only that, but you will start to see others out on the water who clearly could use some pointers. Feel free to help them out.

Lastly, as parting words I will say that wakeboarding is an extremely fun and rewarding activity. It can be frustrating at times, especially while learning, but the feeling of finally getting up or landing that trick you have been practicing is second to none and well worth the effort. Happy riding!

<u>Trick Checklist</u>

Trick Name-Date Attempted-Date Completed

<u>1.</u>

<u>2</u>

<u>3</u>

<u>4</u>

<u>5</u>

<u>6</u>

<u>7</u>

<u>8</u>

<u>9</u>

<u>10</u>

<u>11</u>

<u>12</u>

<u>13</u>

<u>14</u>

<u>15</u>

Made in United States
North Haven, CT
16 November 2024

60427437R00065